D1523502

# DIRT BIKES

KENNY ABDO

## abdopublishing.com

Published by Abdo Zoom, a division of ABDO, P.O. Box 398166, Minneapolis, Minnesota 55439. Copyright © 2018 by Abdo Consulting Group, Inc. International copyrights reserved in all countries. No part of this book may be reproduced in any form without written permission from the publisher.

Printed in the United States of America, North Mankato, Minnesota.
092017
012018

THIS BOOK CONTAINS
RECYCLED MATERIALS

Photo Credits: AP Images, iStock, Shutterstock
Production Contributors: Kenny Abdo, Jennie Forsberg, Grace Hansen
Design Contributors: Dorothy Toth, Neil Klinepier

## Publisher's Cataloging-in-Publication Data

Names: Abdo, Kenny, author.
Title:  Dirt bikes / by Kenny Abdo.
Description: Minneapolis, Minnesota: Abdo Zoom, 2018. | Series: Off road vehicles
      Includes online resource and index.
Identifiers: LCCN 2017939270 | ISBN 9781532121005 (lib.bdg.)
      ISBN 9781532122125 (ebook) | ISBN 9781532122682 (Read-to-Me ebook)
Subjects: LCSH: Dirt Bike--Juvenile literature. | Vehicles--Juvenile literature.
      Motor Sports--Juvenile literature.
Classification: DDC 629.2275--dc23
LC record available at https://lccn.loc.gov/2017939270

# TABLE OF CONTENTS

# DIRT BIKES

A dirt bike is an off-road motorcycle. It is easy to drive over all types of land.

It has a very lightweight frame, which helps riders move around easily.

# TYPES

The first known dirt bike was believed to be made in 1897. The first Motocross race was held in the United Kingdom in 1924.

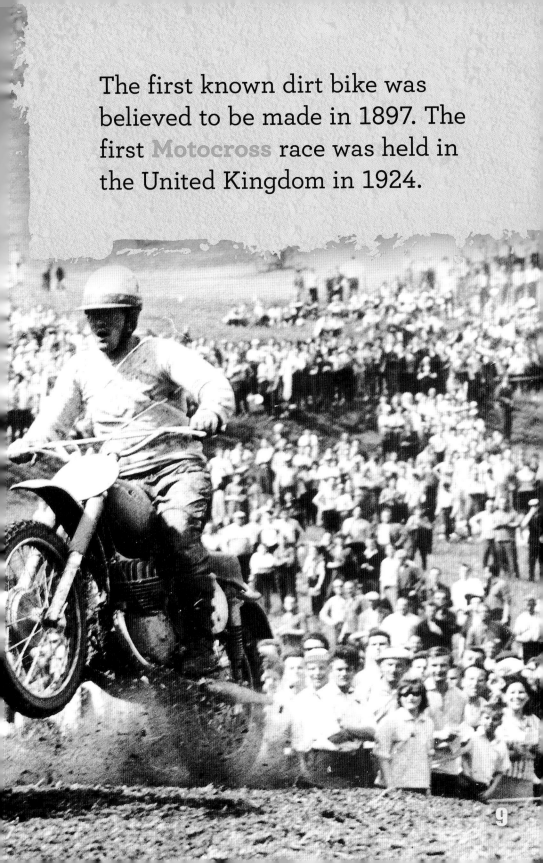

A dirt bike has stiffer suspension than other bikes. This helps take jumps at higher speeds. Its longer forks help get more distance on jumps.

FORK

Dirt bikes also have knobby tires for better grip on terrain like dirt. The bikes sit higher up to ride over rough terrain.

Dirt bikes are illegal to use on streets and highways. They can only be ridden off-road.

Going off-road includes surfaces like gravel, sand, snow, or mud. Off-road tracks can have obstacles as well.

Dirt bikes are
used in Motocross.
It is one of the most
popular sports in the world.

Dirt bikes are used in Motocross because they are light and fast! It helps that they have very small engines.

# GLOSSARY

**engine** – a machine that changes power into motion.

**Motocross** – form of off-road racing with motorcycles on enclosed tracks.

**off-road** – riding a vehicle on difficult roads or tracks, like sand, mud, or gravel.

**suspension** – a system of devices that supports the upper part of an automobile on its axles.

**terrain** – a piece of land having certain features.

**tires** – rubber filled with air that goes over a rim of a wheel.

# ONLINE RESOURCES

**Booklinks**
**NONFICTION NETWORK**
FREE! ONLINE NONFICTION RESOURCES

To learn more about dirt bikes, please visit abdobooklinks.com. These links are routinely monitored and updated to provide the most current information available.

# INDEX